D1174830

The Rutan Voyager

THE GREAT ADVENTURES SERIES
The Rutan Voyager

Ian Goold

Rourke Enterprises, Inc.
Vero Beach, Florida 32964

Jeana Yeager at the controls of
the Rutan Voyager.

LIBRARY OF CONGRESS
Library of Congress Cataloging-in-Publication Data

Goold, Ian, 1951-
  The Rutan Voyager/By Ian Goold

  p. cm. — (Great adventure series)
  Includes index.
  Summary: Describes the planning and historic flight of the airplane Voyager, which carried Richard Rutan and Jeana Yeager in the first nonstop flight around the world without refueling.
  ISBN 0-86592-869-X
  1. Voyager (Airplane) — Juvenile literature.
2. Rutan, Richard — Journeys — Juvenile literature. 3. Yeager, Jeana — Journeys — Juvenile literature. 4. Flights around the world — Juvenile literature. [1. Voyager (Airplane) 2. Rutan, Richard. 3. Yeager, Jeana. 4. Flights around the world.]
I. Title.   II. Series:
G445.G66   1988   88-5969
910.4'1 - dc19   CIP
                           AC

CONTENTS

Into the Unknown

If there was one thing that Dick Rutan did not want to do in the flimsy-looking aircraft he was flying, it was to go anywhere near a thunderstorm. That would be a sure recipe for getting into trouble. Even he, a test pilot and former USAF fighter "jock," might not be able to handle it. The rough air could toss the little craft around like a paper tissue caught in the draft of a passing truck.

Another thing he worried about was flying the fragile machine in the dark. A full moon would always give him some sense of aircraft **attitude,** but in the inky blackness he would be robbed of the last help that nature had to offer. He would have to rely on the instruments in the aircraft, a machine in which every ounce of weight was critical.

Now he was just where he did not want to be. He was flying into the thunderstorm at night with no moon to tell him of any change in the aircraft attitude. He would not see the moon changing position through the cockpit window as the Voyager, built to carry out what had been called the last great adventure—to fly around the world non stop and without refueling—changed direction or rolled in the turbulent air.

Rutan would know something was happening, and his skill as a

The Voyager cabin was very small and cramped.

Voyager flies over thick cloud.

pilot would even allow him to guess what it was. Pilots, like race-car drivers, perform literally by the seat of their pants, feeling the changing pressures as different forces act upon the vehicle.

He was not alone. In the cramped rest area in the tiny cabin of the small craft was Jeana Yeager, who had shared his vision, or dream, as he called it. They were in contact with their Mission Control crew at Edwards Air Force Base in California. But only they could fly the Voyager through the storm.

His weather radar told him that there were storm cells all around. Suddenly, without warning, the weather took over. Later, he was able to recall that he felt calm knowing that there was nothing he could do. He had no control.

But just as quickly he discovered that he was back in control. The giant hand of the thunderstorm had let Voyager go.

Almost without thinking, Rutan began to get the frail craft back onto an even keel. In all the testing that had gone into preparation for the world flight (including a record-breaking mission up and down the Californian coast to prove Voyager's amazing fuel efficiency), he had never rolled the aircraft through more than 20°. Now he knew that Voyager was far beyond that. The fuel in the wings would be sloshing around, upsetting the balance and making it harder for him to keep control.

He hated to think what the wings were doing; they were so slender, thinner even than many sailplanes. The wingtips more than 60 feet away from where he sat would be moving through enormous distances—perhaps as much as 20 feet above or below their normal cruising position.

Len Snellman, chief meteorologist, monitors weather conditions.

Voyager's slender wings were filled with fuel.

Voyager continued to roll until it had gone over an unbelievable 90° — the wings were now vertical, pointing straight up and straight down. This was certainly the end. He told Jeana that they were not going to make it.

Dick Rutan knew that to recover to a normal position he could not just roll the other way. Voyager's flimsy wings were twisting under the load and rolling the craft even further the wrong way. He had to dive. Gently pushing the control stick forward, as if to lower the nose in normal flight, he also pushed the rudder controls to steer the craft. Then slowly, so slowly, he moved the stick a little to the side to level the wings.

Now he was diving at 20° — again more than ever before. A little back pressure on the stick and the nose began steadily to rise. Opening the throttle, he increased engine power to allow Voyager to regain height.

He radioed Control to report the amazing trouble they had had. Since taking off from California, they had flown west right across the Pacific and Indian Oceans, across Africa, and were now almost right across the Atlantic, well into their sixth day. Dick and Jeana's thoughts were increasingly of home. Surely the elements were not going to consume them now, after they had come so far together?

The Ultimate Dream

No one knows who first had the idea to fly around the world. It is perhaps the ultimate dream this side of space. Four hundred years have passed since man first sailed around the world. Nearly 70 years ago, U.S. Navy aircraft were the first to fly completely around, but they made several stops. To fly around non stop and unrefueled was going to be something else entirely.

Dick Rutan and his brother Burt have been infatuated with

At work on Voyager in the Rutan Aircraft Factory.

A view through Voyager's fuselage shows the tiny cabin area.

aircraft, designing or flying them all their lives. Burt had made a name for himself as a youngster flying radio-controlled models. Later he helped the USAF to overcome a problem with its famed F-4 Phantom bomber. Dick has flown fighters in the war in southeast Asia, having begun his service career as a navigator.

In the mid-1970s, Burt set up the Rutan Aircraft Factory in California. Dick went to work for him as a pilot to test the radical designs which Burt was producing.

Burt was very taken with the new **composite materials** that were proving to be both much lighter and stronger than the aluminum alloys with which aircraft had been made for many years.

He liked to come up with designs that challenged established ideas, thinking through problems to find a different and unexpected solution.

Composites can be produced in very smooth shapes, giving added strength and more efficient aerodynamics than metal designs. In his search for high efficiency, Burt had adopted **canard** designs. In this design, the horizontal stabilizer and elevator are at the front of the plane, rather than at the back near the tail as on most aircraft. At the front they balanced the aircraft while contributing to the total lift, allowing the main wing to be smaller. The whole aircraft was lighter and needed less fuel to power it.

One of Burt's first designs was the Vari Eze. This employed many of the classic Rutan hallmarks: rear engine driving a pusher propeller,

Voyager's wings spanned over 110 feet, although the total length of the aircraft was only about 25 feet.

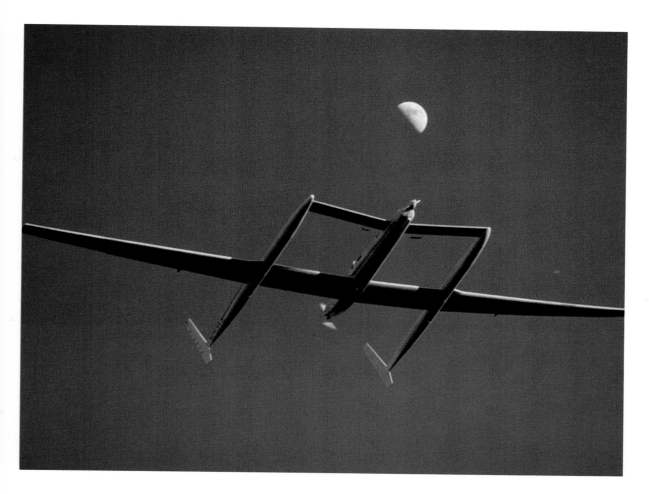

Voyager on a four and one-half
day test flight in July 1986.
This photo was taken at night.

composite construction, canard layout, and **winglets** (small fins at
the wingtips to improve efficiency). This was followed by a two-seat
version called the Long EZ.

Dick took this aircraft to Chino, California, in 1980 for an airshow.
He flew it to show off its shape and to impress the crowd with his
aerobatics.

One of the spectators there was a young woman named Jeana
Yeager. They met and became friends. Before long, Jeana had joined
the Rutan family in California. After a while Jeana and Dick decided
to set up shop, building some of Burt's designs. Talking about this
over lunch in a restaurant in Mojave, Burt challenged them with an
often discussed topic: how about building an aircraft to fly around
the world non stop and without refueling?

Burt sketched a few lines on a paper napkin, and Voyager was
born. That incident soon became famous as the world got word of
their ambitious idea. The very first design was abandoned in favor of a
catamaran that Burt had had in mind for some time. It became
known as Rutan Model 76.

Long Flights Need Long Take-offs

Voyager is an aircraft of "gee-whiz" numbers. Most of its characteristics are extreme when compared with conventional aircraft. It weighed less than 1,000 pounds structurally, yet it would have to carry more than seven times that amount of fuel. Although its wings spanned more than 110 feet, the aircraft measured just over 25 feet from front to back. It would need almost three miles of runway for take-off.

Jeana Yeager packs up the provisions for the flight.

Jeana and Dick on the morning
of the flight.

The crew had been warned that when a good opportunity came
for their attempt to do what had not been done before, they should
go for it, even if conditions were not ideal: "The airplane will never be
totally ready; the weather will never be as good as you want it."

Now as they prepared for the flight itself, they could hardly believe
just how quickly things had happened, finally. Once they had done all
they could, it was up to the weatherman. The whole team would meet
at ten o'clock each morning, and if things looked good Voyager
would be flown to Edwards Air Force Base and readied for flight
early the next day. Their first-morning meeting was their *only* one:
they decided to go.

Some 22 hours later they were in Voyager and feeling calmer than
they expected to. The ground crew had spent much of the night
fueling her very slowly through the model-aircraft filler caps that
weighed little and permitted almost no leakage. Each gallon had been
logged and Dick Rutan had insisted on adding 300 pounds more.

A little after 8 A.M., Rutan released the brake and slowly eased the throttles open. The crew concentrated on every aspect as Voyager accelerated. They had never flown her this heavy and did not know how it would feel. They knew that at first the wingtips would scrape on the ground until they slowly began to rise as the wing generated lift.

Rutan watched for distance markers on the runway and matched them to speeds which Jeana read off from the airspeed indicator. At the third marker they had agreed they would abort if the speed was more than 3 knots down. It was 4 knots below the target speed; but they carried on, knowing they had insufficient runway in which to stop.

What they did *not* know was that the wingtips were not rising as they should have. This was slowing them. In the **chase plane** flying right alongside at no more than 15 feet from the ground, Burt Rutan

Voyager's crew status is recorded prior to take-off from Edwards Air Force Base.

Take-off! December 14, 1986.

thought they had a control problem. Perhaps Dick could not pull back far enough on the control stick to lift the nose at this greater weight. He shouted over the radio: "Pull the stick back."

Voyager had gone well past two miles and still their speed was too low. As Dick eased (not pulled - just eased) back on the stick, the wings finally began to lift. The tips left the ground and instead of sagging down they now rose to form a graceful arch on each side, much higher than Dick and Jeana had ever seen them. Voyager eventually left the ground a half-mile later. The record would show that the take-off had taken 14,200 feet, almost three miles.

Dick held the aircraft low in what pilots call ground effect—within a wingspan of the ground—where lift is enhanced, until they reached the magic 100 knots speed they wanted for climb. Perhaps the most relieved was one of their crew who watched from the runway and thought they would not make it: "I thought they were going to fireball."

Don't Be Concerned, But ---

The great adventure, perhaps the last great adventure left within the atmosphere of Earth, was under way. Adjusting the control stick to maintain an even speed. Dick checked the climb rate. It was 300 feet per minute, more than double the figure they expected.

He pulled the T-handle that retracted the nosewheel. Jeana would operate the cable that raised the mainwheels. They flew a lazy half-circle to bring them back over Edwards should they need an emergency landing soon after take-off.

As they flew over they received a radio message from the chase plane: "Don't be concerned, but the right winglet has failed." The device, which is used to influence the air as it flows over and around

Burt Rutan watches Voyager closely from a chase plane.

Dick Rutan at the controls of Voyager.

the wingtip, effectively increasing span and reducing drag, was hanging loose.

Now Dick knew why speed had risen so slowly on take-off. The winglets had been dragging on the runway — for nearly three miles. To those on the ground, the white dust which had erupted from the dragging tips seemed as though it might be spray from a fuel leak. What had gone wrong?

It was a little while before they realized that there were three reasons. To prevent the inboard wing generating more lift than the tips, the nosewheel leg had been shortened a little. This meant that the air struck the wing at a slightly different angle.

Then to improve wingtip clearance at the beginning of the take-off run, the pressure in the main landing-gear legs had been increased. Finally, extra fuel had been put in the forward tanks, weighing the nose down even more.

All this meant that instead of rising quickly as lift build up, the wing actually flew *downwards* toward the runway because the nose was so low.

What would all this mean for the record flight? Without the lift from that wingtip could they stay in the air? Would the drag slow them down? More important, would it increase their fuel consumption too much so that they could not make it before running out of gas?

Could Dick still control the aircraft? He confirmed that he could; using each of the controls in turn he found all was in order. To see if there was a fuel leak, the chase plane flew in close behind them, but no, there was no tell-tale fuel mist on the windshield. This was a concern, since fuel vents ran through the winglets. All seemed OK.

So, what about the two damaged winglets now helplessly attached

There was not much room for navigation inside Voyager's cramped cabin.

This photo shows how Voyager's wings bend upward in flight.

by slivers of material? At first Burt Rutan in the chaseplane thought of literally knocking them off — with the wing of *his* plane! But Dick would not hear of it. The disturbed airflow around the two aircraft as they flew close together could easily upset Voyager, causing a collision.

They decided to try to shake the winglets loose by putting Voyager into a **sideslip**. First, they would have to get high enough to parachute to safety if things went wrong.

After putting on their parachutes Dick applied right rudder to sideslip, figuring that it was best for the winglet to go outboard. If it came inboard the skin might just peel off and rupture the fuel tank.

He tried again with more force, after Burt suggested more speed was needed. The winglet shook, moving fore and aft at the end of the flimsy wing, before sailing away. The top skin was torn back to the fuel tank leaving just the wires that had gone to the wingtip lights trailing in the air. If they touched there could be a spark. Dick disconnected the electrical power and hoped he had not lost anything else.

21

Flying Through The Storm

Since they needed to conserve fuel, their climb had to be as shallow as possible. They had only to clear high ground by a reasonable margin and their course took them through Soledad Pass where Highway 14 cuts through on its way to Los Angeles.

Other aircraft ahead of them checked for any **turbulence** in the air over the mountain ridges. Dick and Jeana were tossed around as they crossed, and for once in his life Dick found himself looking forward to flying out over the ocean where it would be smooth. He began to weaken the gas mixture, stopping the climb at almost 6,000 feet. Two hours after take-off they crossed the California coast near Oxnard, checking their navigation equipment as they did so. It was the last chance before reaching Hawaii.

In the chase plane, Burt Rutan worked out the implications of the lost wingtips. With extra drag around the rough ends of the wing and from the torn skin hanging off, he reckoned range would be cut by no more than 6 percent, perhaps 1,500 miles. But fuel consumption was looking good. They were flying more than $2\frac{1}{2}$ miles on each pound of fuel they burned; that is about 20 miles per gallon. Now they were alone. The chase plane turned for home; it was already running low on fuel, but Dick and Jeana had more than 25,000 miles to go without refueling.

A few hours before they reached Hawaii, the sun went down for the first time. It was to go down seven more times before they landed. They were to operate on Julian time, which ignores months, just numbering days of the year from January 1. Jeana was to lose all track of time. They used Greenwich Mean Time (based on the actual time in London) for all purposes, it was hard to keep track of what time it was in California and what time it was where they were flying.

Burt Rutan monitors the flight from Mojave, California.

Sunset over Hawaii — the first of seven sunsets.

They were met by a chase plane from Hawaii, but confusion over rendezvous arrangements meant an hour-long tail chase for their companions, who stayed nearby briefly before heading back.

Jeana began to establish the daily routine that was designed to make sure they maintained a proper regime. On their record-breaking coastal flight she had suffered from **dehydration**, so she made sure that she drank plenty. Everything was in premeasured packs. Jeana ate mostly crackers and peanut butter, she reported later, while Dick preferred **Yurika meals** heated in the cramped cockpit. He like to extend his meal times, but Jeana would hurry him so that sudden turbulence, for example, would not cause a spill. Dick flew Voyager for the first three days. Sometimes he was able to sleep briefly for up to an hour, with Jeana watching the controls over his shoulder. But this was the way it had to be until they had used up a

Dense clouds gather under the Rutan Voyager.

lot of their fuel. If they thought that their trip was going to be straightforward, Marge had other ideas. Before leaving California, they had been advised that a storm was brewing in the Pacific. This was good and bad news. Good because as the strong winds swept around the storm—named Marge by the weathermen—Voyager would benefit from good tailwinds; bad because they had to fly close to the storm, which meant that the frail craft would be tossed around.

The weathermen back in California watched the satellite pictures to keep track of Marge, which moved faster than expected. Voyager

would run right into it as it pushed north across their track heading for the Phillipines.

Voyager's weather radar showed large red patches, a sure sign of storm clouds. Huge banks of cloud could be seen through the small windows but the flight was smoother than expected.

Their weathermen said that they were between two spokes of the **cloudwheel** surrounding Marge. They got their tailwinds, but for the first time they met rain. As the sun went down they were under cloud without a star to steer by.

With Marge behind them they might have expected to relax, but it was not to be. The autopilot was about to fail. Sudden loss of this could mean that there might only be a few seconds in which to stabilize the aircraft. Any longer and Voyager would go out of contol very easily. Fortunately a problem during early testing had given an opportunity for them to anticipate such an event. They had practiced replacing the gear.

Dick in the pilot seat had to get his legs out of the way so that Jeana could wriggle under the panel to unplug the equipment and put the wires onto the spare unit.

Back in California Burt was worried about fuel consumption. The numbers he was getting back from Voyager's crew suggested that there was a huge leak. They considered advising a landing in the Phillipines.

Voyager was by now being flown on just one engine, as had been the plan. Over Thailand they spoke to their ground crew who had flown across the Pacific hoping to meet them in the air. They were unable to arrange a plane but watched Voyager's anti-collision beacon as it flew over. Any inspection of the damaged wingtips would have to wait until they were over Africa.

Out over the Indian Ocean beyond the Malay Peninsula they ran into bad weather again, continuing to hit the **Intertropical Convergence Zone**, a group of storms that runs round the world. Trying to climb over huge thunder clouds Dick found he was flying too slowly, almost stalling. Going down to get more speed, he was back in cloud.

Flying further north than planned to avoid the worst, they crossed Sri Lanka. Now they also began to worry about their fuel burn. Voyager was much lighter, but they were getting only four miles per pound of fuel. The support team began to plan to recover the aircraft should it land in Grenada, or Ascension, or Trinidad...or Puerto Rico. In fact no one knew where they might have to land. This problem was offset a little when they passed a point approaching Africa, which meant that they had set a new record, flying farther than anyone had before.

Fuel To Spare

Then almost simultaneously Dick and Jeana and the ground crew worked out where all the fuel was going—back into the tanks! Dick looked down at a fuel line in the cockpit and saw the bubbles going wrong way. Studying the fuel system design in California, an engineer figured that fuel flowing back from the engine was measured by their flow meters as if it had flowed *out* of the tank; it was being measured twice. This explained why so much power had been required at times to climb, they were heavier than their log of fuel use suggested. Now they knew they had enough fuel to cross Africa and the Atlantic. Everyone was overjoyed.

A chase plane came up from Nairobi and by comparing their climb rate and power settings Dick and Jeana worked out the Voyager's weight and therefore fuel load. They were right where the predictions said they should be. As they crossed the coast to go out over the Atlantic they both wept.

Safely across the Atlantic and the north part of South America, fate still held what Dick later called "another curve ball." With just over a thousand miles to fly, they gleaned fuel from each of the tanks in turn. The left tip tank was almost empty. Three quarters of its fuel had gone.

Dick discovered that a fuel transfer pump was not working. He went ahead using the engine's mechanical pump, switching tanks as each one drained before the engine quit. While talking weather with California, he did not notice the fuel flow stop. Then the engine stopped.

Dick pushed the nose down hoping to use airspeed to turn the prop enough to draw fuel through and restart the engine. He could tell from the moon that they were turning as they descended.

A photo of Dick Rutan taken by the onboard camera.

Crossing the coast of California on the return leg of the journey.

They went through the checklist for airstarting the engine. Voyager was losing height rapidly. At 3,500 feet the front engine started. As soon as he levelled out, Jeana told Dick that the rear engine started. Well, of course, it would: with the nose up fuel would flow back into it! They should have known, but fatigue was taking its toll as they entered the last lap, almost eight full days after take-off.

This close to home they kept the front engine running. At the lower altitude there was less headwind.

Soon they knew that the chase plane had taken off to meet them. To avoid being "buzzed" by amateur pilots, Voyager flew off the coast to make a straight run into Edwards. Light snow was falling there, and a constant stream of carlights entered the base. The American public came to show their appreciation of a great effort and a great adventure. Dick and Jeana had fuel for solo flybys before landing. Voyager landed with only 12 gallons of fuel remaining, just over nine days after they had left.

Once Dick and Jeana had worked out where they were required to park their flimsy craft on the huge Edwards base, they taxied Voyager to the spot. A large crowd had gathered, and photographers and TV crews were waiting to greet the intrepid pair.

For record verification purposes, the canopy seals were inspected. Then the canopy was opened, and they got their first breath of fresh air in nine days. Dick climbed out and sat for a little while astride the fuselage. He worried that his legs, which had felt okay in the cabin, might not work when he stood up. But they did work, and both Dick and Jeana were able to walk around and check the aircraft before going for medical checks at the base hospital.

The medical checks showed that Jeana had lost 9 pounds and Dick 6 pounds. They both went home after a small celebration with their crew and supporters. They were too tired for the large party that they had promised themselves. Dick slept for 18 hours straight, but Jeana managed only 8 hours. She was back in the office as usual first thing the next morning.

Checks on the aircraft showed that they had landed with just 1.5 percent of their fuel remaining and that Jeana's fuel log was accurate to within 20 pounds. The project had left them almost a half million dollars in debt, and they soon set off on a round of speechmaking and lecturing to recoup their costs.

Only afterwards did they realize how much the project had attracted world attention. Jeana's vision of Voyager bringing together one world with one flight came true. At the end of a year which had begun with the loss of the *Challenger* crew, Dick and Jeana had given America a big Christmas gift. Asked if they would do it again, they say: "No one can do it again. That is the best thing about it."

Thousands of spectators turned out at Edwards Air Force Base to welcome home Dick, Jeana, and Voyager.

Dick Rutan and Jeana Yeager became the first people to fly non-stop around the world without refueling.

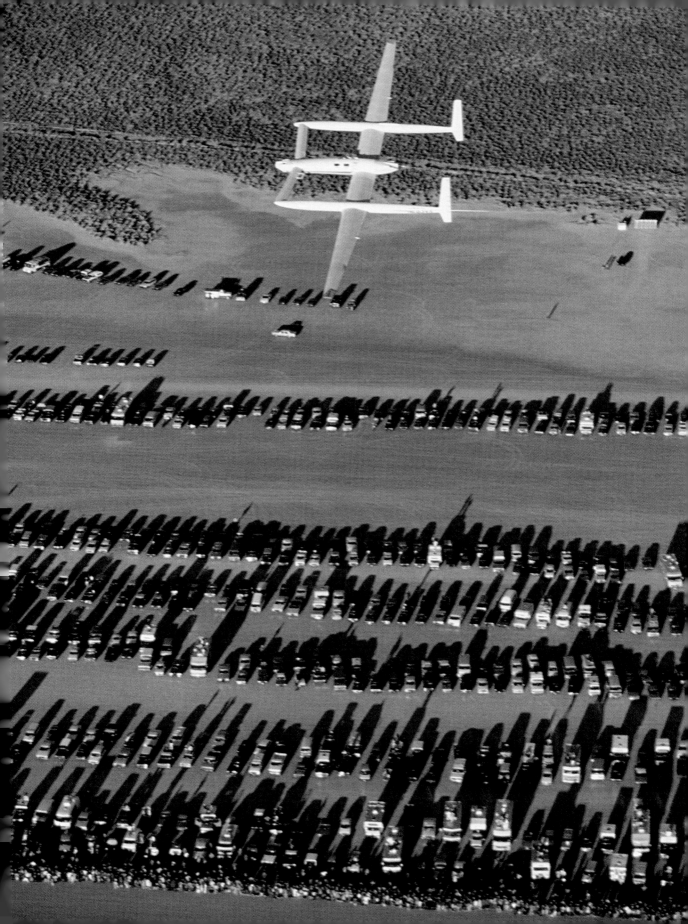

Glossary

Attitude	An aircraft's position in the air when flying. For example, an aircraft can be controlled to fly "nose high" or "one wing low" while maintaining straight level flight.
Composite Material	A kind of material formed of threads of carbon or fibre set in plastic resin, claimed to be both lighter and stronger than metal.
Catamaran	A style of boat having two identical side-by-side hulls for extra stability. Voyager's two long fuel tanks give a similar appearance.
Chase Plane	Any aircraft used to observe another in flight, usually for photography or, less commonly, as an escort.
Cloudwheel	The arrangement of clouds around the eye of a storm, especially seen from above and in weather satellite photographs.
Dehydration	Loss of body fluid through prolonged exposure to dry air. All long-distance air travelers in pressurized, air-conditioned cabins and all who live in air-conditioned environments suffer some degree of dehydration.
Inter-Tropical Convergence Zone	The area between the Tropics that contains a band of storms encircling the world.
Sideslip	An aircraft's equivalent of a car skidding. The craft does not point in the direction of travel.
Turbulence	Rough air caused by previous passage of an aircraft, a draft thrown up (or down) off a hillside by wind, or by heated air rising from ground.
Winglets	Also called tipsails, these are small extensions like tail fins on wingtips to reduce drag and provide additional forward force.
Yurika meals	The trade name of dry meals prepared by adding water and heat.

RUTAN VOYAGER

Index